Home Starts Here:

A First-Time Home Buyer's Guide for Women Over 40

By Robin DeFleice

Copyright 2025 Robin DeFleice

All rights reserved. No part of this publication may be reproduced or distributed without written permission of the author.

Printed in the United States of America

This book is a work of personal insight and experience. It is not intended to be a substitute for professional advice.

Dedication To The DeFleice Family and friend Marilyn J Brown. In memory of: My mother Barbara Ann DeFleice, and Grandmother Queen Ester Edwards. Acknowledgments to:

Jermaine Brooks, team lead for the List Sell Buy Team.

Table of Contents

Introduction
Chapter 1: Why Now Is the Right Time
Chapter 2: Getting Mentally & Financially Ready
Chapter 3: Renting vs. Buying in Your 40s, 50s, and 60s
Chapter 4: Step-by-Step Guide to the Home Buying Process
Chapter 5: Budgeting for Your First Home
Chapter 6: Creating a Support Circle
Chapter 7: The Full Journey-From Pre-Approval to Keys
Chapter 8: After Closing - Settling In and Owning with Confidence
Chapter 9: Making the Most of Your Home

Appendices

Glossary of Real Estate Terms A

Budget Worksheet B

First-Time Buyer's Checklist C

Introduction

My Journey to Homeownership at 66 - and Why It's Never Too Late for You

At 67 years old, I'm living proof that it's never too late to own your first home, change your life, or start a brand-new chapter.

I didn't buy my first home in my 30s or 40s like so many others. I signed the closing documents on my very first house in August 2023. On January 10, 2025, I became a licensed real estate agent. Just a few months later, I retired from a short but meaningful career as a mental health case manager.

For most of my life, I rented. I worked hard, I took college classes and walked through seasons of heartbreak and financial setbacks. I lost my mother at 50. I moved to Texas during the 2008 housing crash with little more than hope and a suitcase. I returned to Cleveland in 2013 to rebuild, one step at a time. I earned my associate's degree at 62, and my bachelor's at 64. I became a notary. I worked full-time supporting others through life's challenges-and I saw time and again how housing instability impacted nearly every aspect of a person's well-being.

Still, for a long time, I didn't believe homeownership was possible for me.

Then something shifted. I realized I had spent a lot of time helping others find safety, healing, and stability. I deserved those things, too.

This book is for women like me-women who may have taken the long way home. Women who put others first. Women who believed the opportunity had passed them by. Women who've weathered loss, divorce, career changes, or fresh starts. Whether you're 40, 50, or well into your 60s, hear me clearly: you are not too old, and it is not too late.

You deserve to own your space. To build wealth and create a legacy. To hang your family photos without worrying about a landlord. To walk into a house and say, "This is mine."

In this guide, I'll walk you through every step of buying your first home-from getting financially prepared, to understanding the real estate process, to what to expect after you get the keys. Along the way, I'll share stories from my own journey, and give you the same tools I now use as a real estate agent and former case manager.

This isn't just a how-to manual. It's a yes-you-can guidebook.

And I'll be with you, every step of the way.

Let's get started-your home, and your fresh start, are waiting.

- Robin DeFleice

First-time homeowner. Real estate agent. Proud woman over 60.

Chapter 1: Why Now Is the Right Time

You're Not Too Old-You're Right on Time

If you're reading this and thinking, "I should have done this years ago," stop right there.

Buying a home isn't about being early or late. It's about being ready. And readiness has nothing to do with age it has everything to do with intention, preparation, and the courage to take a step forward.

I bought my first home at 66. For years, I didn't think homeownership was something for me. I didn't have children to pass it down to. I'd been a renter all my life, and while the thought of owning a home crossed my mind, it never seemed urgent-until it was.

What pushed me to seriously consider buying a home was the rent. It kept rising year after year.

I looked at the numbers and started asking, Could I be paying less if I owned something? Could I actually save money and invest in myself? The answer surprised me: yes.

And once I saw that, I knew it was time to make a change.

The Myth of "Too Late"

There's a false belief out there that if you haven't bought a home by your 30s or 40s, you've missed your chance. That myth keeps many women stuck in place. Here's the truth:

You can still qualify for a mortgage in your 40s, 50s, and 60s.

You can build equity and financial security at any age.

You can create a stable, personalized living space that reflects who you are right now.

Life doesn't always go in a straight line. Maybe you prioritized education, cared for a loved one, survived setbacks, or just didn't have the resources earlier. None of that disqualifies you from becoming a homeowner.

The Advantages of Buying Later in Life

There are actually benefits to becoming a homeowner in your 40s and beyond:

More clarity. You know what you want in a home-and what you don't want.

Better budgeting skills. You've had time to build discipline with your finances. Emotional readiness. You value stability and security over trends or pressure.

Life wisdom. You've lived enough life to know that home is more than walls and windows-it's peace, independence, and pride of ownership.

When I decided to stop renting, it wasn't about chasing a dream-it was about claiming my stability. I wanted to stop giving money to landlords and start investing in myself.

You're Not Alone

According to the National Association of Realtors, more single women over 40 are buying homes than ever before. We are one of the fastest-growing segments of homebuyers.

You don't need a spouse, children, or a big inheritance. What you need is clarity, support, and a willingness to believe that you're worth the investment. That's what this book is here to provide. Let's Get Practical

Here's a preview of what we'll cover in the next chapters:

How to prepare financially

Understanding credit and what lenders look for

Creating a personalized homebuying timeline

Building your support team

Choosing a home that fits your life-not someone else's expectations but before we move forward, remember this:

You are not behind. You are right on time.

You're not too old. You're just getting started.

And the best time to begin? Is now.

Next up: In Chapter 2, we'll talk about getting mentally and financially ready-because homeownership starts long before you walk through a front door.

Chapter 2: Getting Mentally & Financially Ready

From Doubt to Determination - Preparing Yourself for the Journey Ahead

When I first started thinking seriously about buying a home, I wasn't just worried about the money-I was worried about me.

Was I too old to start this?

Would I be approved?

What if I made the wrong decision?

Those thoughts were loud in my head. I had spent years working as a mental health case manager, supporting clients who were constantly battling unstable housing, eviction notices, poor living conditions, or living doubled-up with family. I saw firsthand how much housing affects every part of someone's life-mental health, finances, family relationships, and self-worth.

But even as I advocated for them to find safe and stable homes, I hadn't done that for myself. I hadn't believed it was possible. And yet, deep down, I knew: if I wanted something different, I had to believe I was worth investing in.

This chapter is about building that belief-for you. Whether your journey is just starting or you're halfway there, it's time to prepare your mindset and your money. Because when your heart and head are in the right place, the rest will follow.

Step 1: Get Your Mind Right

Whether you're 42 or 67, first-time homebuying can stir up insecurities. You might feel late to the game. You might not feel "qualified." Maybe no one in your family ever owned a home. That's okay.

Here's what to remind yourself:

You don't need to have it all figured out-just take the next step.

You deserve peace, pride, and personal space.

You've overcome far more than a loan application.

Buying a home is a personal transformation. I've seen people's lives change once they had a safe, stable place to call their own. I've seen it in my clients, and now I've lived it myself.

✦Affirmation: I am worthy of ownership, stability, and a space that's mine.

Step 2: Start With the Money You Have

You don't need a huge savings account to begin. What you do need is a clear picture of your finances and a realistic plan. Here's how to start:

✓Track Your Current Expenses

Print out your last two months of bank statements. Highlight every expense: rent, food, gas, subscriptions, etc. What can you reduce or eliminate? How much can you begin saving?

✓Know Your Credit Score

Your credit score plays a huge role in getting approved for a mortgage. If you don't know yours, start with a free service like Credit Karma or request a free report from AnnualCreditReport.com.

Scores generally fall into these ranges:

720+ = Excellent

680-719 = Good

620-679 = Fair (still often approved)

Below 620 = Challenging but not impossible

Don't be discouraged by a low score-there are ways to improve it, and some lenders offer programs for lower-credit buyers.

✓ Set a Savings Goal

While there are programs that allow for low down payments, you'll still need money for:

Earnest money (1-2% of the purchase price)

Inspections and appraisal

Closing costs (2-5% of the home price)

Moving and setup costs

Even saving $100-$200 a month can add up quickly. It shows discipline and helps you build a habit of "paying yourself first."

Step 3: Educate Yourself

Knowledge reduces fear. The more you understand how the homebuying process works, the more empowered you'll feel. You're already starting by reading this book. Here are a few more ways to stay informed:

Watch videos (like on my YouTube channel!)

Attend free homebuyer workshops

Follow trusted real estate professionals on social media

Talk to a lender early-even if you're not ready to buy yet

You don't have to wait until everything is perfect. Preparation is part of the process.

Step 4: Build Your Confidence Toolkit

Here are a few tools that will help you feel grounded along the way:

Budget worksheet (included in the appendix)

Homebuyer checklist

A simple journal to track your thoughts, wins, and setbacks

Supportive people who encourage your journey-not those who cast doubt

Be Patient, But Persistent

Not everyone is ready to buy tomorrow-and that's okay. You might need a few months to get things in order. But every small step you take today is an investment in your future.

"A year from now, you'll wish you had started today."

You're not just preparing your wallet-you're preparing your worth. And the woman who is ready to buy a home is already inside you. This chapter is about meeting her.

Next up: In Chapter 3, we'll explore whether it's better to rent or buy at this stage in your life-and how to decide what's best for you, right now.

Chapter 3: Renting vs. Buying in Your 40s, 50s, and 60s Is It Really Cheaper to Buy? Let's Break It Down.

If you're like I was, you may have spent years-maybe decades-renting. At first, it was convenient. No maintenance worries. No long-term commitment. But over time, the price of that convenience started to creep higher and higher.

For me, it wasn't a dream of a white-picket fence that got me thinking about buying a home-it was the rent hikes. Every year, my rent crept up. And every year, I was giving away money with nothing to show for it. Eventually, I started wondering: Could I actually be spending less by owning a home?

This chapter will help you answer that question for yourself. We'll walk through the pros and cons of renting and buying later in life, and help you figure out when buying makes sense for your lifestyle, finances, and future.

Why Women Over 40 Reevaluate Housing

When we're younger, we tend to follow housing paths based on jobs, relationships, and family responsibilities. But once we reach our 40s, 50s, and 60s, priorities change. We're looking for:

Stability and security

Fixed, predictable housing costs

The ability to personalize our space

A long-term financial plan

And let's be honest-many of us are tired of the uncertainty that comes with renting. Your lease could go up. The landlord could sell the building. You might not be able to hang a picture without permission.

For many women, this stage of life is the perfect time to take control-and owning a home is one powerful way to do that.

The Financial Side: Renting vs. Owning Let's break down the big differences:

Keep in mind:

Renting may cost less month-to-month in some areas.

But buying helps you build wealth through equity.

As a homeowner, you can qualify for tax deductions, such as mortgage interest and property taxes (check with a tax advisor).

And while buying does have upfront costs, many programs help reduce or spread those out (we'll cover that later).

A Real-World Example

Let's say your rent is $1,200/month. That's $14,400 per year.

If you own a home with a $1,100 monthly mortgage, and that included taxes and insurance, you could actually save money and be investing in something that belongs to you.

Over 5 years:

Renting = $72,000 paid to someone else

Owning = $66,000 paid into your future, plus equity, plus potential home appreciation Now imagine you stay for 10 or 15 years. That's a major shift in your financial future. But What If I'm Not Ready to Settle Down?

Buying doesn't mean you're locked into one place forever. You can always sell or even rent out your home later. But the key difference is you're in control.

Renting may offer short-term flexibility, but homeownership gives you long-term options.

Ask Yourself:

Is my rent going up every year?

Do I want more control over my living space?

Could I stay in the same place for at least 5 years?

Would a fixed payment give me peace of mind?

Am I tired of paying for something I'll never own?

If you answered yes to most of these, it may be time to start thinking seriously about buying.

Next Steps

Don't worry, we're not rushing into anything. This chapter is about opening your eyes to possibility. If you're not ready today, that's okay. But start preparing as if you will be. That way, when the right home comes along-or when your lease renewal hits your
inbox-you're ready to choose powerfully.

Next up: In Chapter 4, we'll take a step-by-step walk through the home buying process, from pre-approval to closing. If you've never done it before, don't worry-I'll be right here to guide you.

Chapter 4: Step-by-Step Guide to the Home Buying Process

From Dreaming to Closing - What Really Happens and When

By now, you're starting to see that buying a home isn't just for the young or the wealthy. It's for you, and it's closer than you think. But even when you feel mentally and financially ready, it can be overwhelming trying to figure out where to begin.

What's a pre-approval?

When do I make an offer?

Do I really need a home inspection?

You're not alone in asking these questions. In this chapter, we'll walk through the home buying process step-by-step, from getting your finances in order to the moment you get your keys. It's not as complicated as it seems-especially when you know what to expect.

☐ Step 1: Get Pre-Approved

Before you even start looking at houses, talk to a mortgage lender. This will help you understand:

How much home can you afford

What kind of loan do you qualify for

What your estimated monthly payments will be

A pre-approval letter shows sellers that you're serious and that you're financially ready. It can also uncover any issues early, like errors in your credit report or documents you still need.

Tip: Ask your real estate agent (like me!) for a list of trusted lenders if you don't already have one.

Step 2: Partner with the Right Real Estate Agent

Your agent will be your guide, advocate, and translator throughout the entire process. A good agent will:

Help you identify the right neighborhoods

Schedule and attend showings with you

Submit offers and negotiate on your behalf

Help you understand the contract and closing process

Ask around-especially among other women who've bought homes-and interview more than one agent if needed. You deserve someone who listens to you, respects your timeline, and explains things clearly.

Step 3: Tour Homes and Make an Offer

Once you've been pre-approved and shared your must-haves with your agent, the fun begins: house hunting!

As you tour homes:

Take notes and photos to remember what you liked

Don't rush, this is a big decision

Listen to your gut, but also your budget

When you find "the one," your agent will help you make an offer based on market conditions, comparable sales, and your comfort zone. Your offer may include:

Purchase price

- Earnest money deposit (good faith money)
- Timeline for inspections and closing
- Contingencies (such as financing, appraisal, or inspection)

Step 4: Schedule a Home Inspection

Once your offer is accepted, schedule a home inspection right away (your agent will help with this). A professional inspector checks the home's condition—from the roof to the foundation.

They'll provide a report that identifies any issues. Depending on what's found, you may:

- Proceed as planned
- Request repairs or credits
- Walk away if the issues are serious and can't be resolved

Tip: Always attend your inspection and ask questions. It's a great opportunity to learn about the home.

Step 5: Apply for Your Mortgage

Even though you're pre-approved, you still need to submit a full loan application after your offer is accepted. Your lender will request:

- Updated income documentation
- Bank statements
- Verification of employment
- Property information

This step also triggers the appraisal, where the lender confirms the home's value supports the loan amount.

Step 6: Final Loan Approval & Closing Disclosure

Once your lender has reviewed everything, you'll receive a Closing Disclosure at least 3 days before closing. This document outlines:

Final loan terms

Monthly payment

Total closing costs

Cash you'll need to bring to closing

✨Review it carefully with your agent or lender. If anything looks off, ask questions!

Step 7: Closing Day

This is the big day! You'll sign final documents, transfer funds, and receive your keys. Most closings take place at a title company or attorney's office and last about an hour.

Bring:

A government-issued photo ID

A cashier's check or proof of wire transfer

Your patience (it's a lot of paperwork but it's worth it!)

When all is said and done, you'll walk out as a homeowner. Yes-you!

扁 What Comes Next?

After closing, you'll:

Change your address

Set up utilities in your name

Register any pets, vehicles, or school children if needed
Move in and make it your own!

We'll go deeper into this in Chapter 7, but for now, take a moment to picture that first night in your new home. You earned it.

Next up: In Chapter 5, we'll talk money-how to create a homebuying budget that works, what hidden costs to plan for, and how to protect yourself from surprise expenses.

Chapter 5: Budgeting for Your First Home

Planning Ahead to Protect Your Peace (and Your Wallet)

Let's talk about money-not from a place of fear, but from a place of power.

One of the biggest things that holds women back from buying their first home isn't credit, or even income-it's the fear of the unknown. "What if I can't afford it? What if something breaks?

What if I end up house-poor?"

I understand those fears because I had them, too. But I also know this: the more I understood the real costs of buying a home, the less scary it felt. Knowledge gave me confidence, and planning gave me peace.

In this chapter, we're going to walk through the key pieces of a first-time buyer's budget-so you can make smart decisions, feel financially secure, and enjoy your new home without second-guessing yourself.

Step 1: Know What You Can Really Afford

Lenders might approve you for more than you actually feel comfortable spending. Just because they say you can afford a $1,500/month mortgage doesn't mean that fits your real budget or lifestyle.

A good rule of thumb: Your mortgage (including taxes and insurance) should be no more than 30% of your monthly income after taxes.

So, if you bring home $3,500/month:

Aim to spend no more than $1,050/month on your mortgage.

This leaves room for:

Utilities

Food

Transportation

Healthcare

Emergencies

Enjoying your life!

Step 2: Prepare for Upfront Costs

You'll need some cash before you ever move in. Here's a breakdown of the most common upfront costs:

Ask your lender and agent if there are first-time buyer programs in your area that can help with down payment or closing cost assistance.

Step 3: Budget for Monthly & Ongoing Costs

Once you're in the home, you'll have new responsibilities that come with the keys. Plan for:

Mortgage payment (includes principal, interest, taxes, insurance)

Utilities (gas, electric, water, sewer, trash)

Internet and phone

Maintenance (routine upkeep like HVAC filters, lawn care, etc.)

Repairs (broken appliance, roof leak, plumbing issues)

A good rule is to set aside 1% of your home's value per year for maintenance and unexpected repairs. So, if your home costs $150,000, budget $1,500/year-or about $125/month-for upkeep.

Step 4: Create Your Home Buying Budget

Let's put it all together. Here's a simple sample budget to help you map things out.

Sample Buyer Profile

Monthly take-home pay: $3,200

Target home price: $140,000

Estimated monthly mortgage: $900

Utilities & internet: $250

Home maintenance savings: $125

Groceries, gas, life: $1,400

Remaining cushion: $525

This buyer can comfortably afford her new home and still maintain her quality of life. And if something breaks, she's prepared-not panicked.

A printable version of this worksheet is included in the Appendix.

Step 5: Be Realistic-Not Restrictive

This isn't about pinching every penny or living in fear. It's about protecting your peace.

A budget isn't punishment. It's freedom. It tells your money where to go, instead of wondering where it went. And when you're a homeowner, a little planning goes a long way toward keeping you confident and in control.

Unexpected but Real Costs to Remember

Here are some small but important costs people often overlook:

New locks and keys for safety

Blinds or curtains (many homes don't include them)

Trash cans, cleaning supplies, basic tools

Lawn mower or snow shovel

An emergency fund-just in case

You don't have to buy everything at once. Start small and build over time. You've waited this long to own your home-you can take your time settling into it.

Next up: In Chapter 6, we'll talk about your support circle-who needs to be on your team, how to ask for help, and how to filter out negativity and noise during this major life transition.

Chapter 6: Creating a Support Circle

I Bought Alone-And That's Exactly Why I'm Writing This Book

When I bought my first home, I didn't have a team. I didn't have someone walking me through the details or helping me avoid costly missteps. I did what I thought was right-I asked questions, I followed instructions, and I trusted my agent to guide me.

But after closing, I realized I hadn't been fully informed. I learned some things, the hard way-things that should have been explained to me up front. Things that could have saved me time, stress, and money.

That experience changed me.

I enrolled in real estate courses-not because I wanted a new career at first, but because I needed to understand what had happened and why. I needed to learn the system, the steps, and the risks. And the more I learned, the more I realized I wasn't alone. Too many women-especially first-time buyers-are going through this process without support, without clarity, and without someone truly advocating for them.

That's why I became a real estate agent.

That's why I'm writing this book.

And that's why I want you to have something I didn't: a strong, informed support circle.

Who Should Be In Your Support Circle?

Even if you're independent (like me), buying a home shouldn't be something you do in isolation.

Here's who you should have on your side:

1. A Real Estate Agent Who Educates You, Not Just Closes You. The right agent doesn't just help you "get the deal done." They:

Explain the risks and red flags

Answer your questions honestly, not sales talk

Help you compare options

Tell you the truth-even if it costs them the sale

✦This is the kind of agent I decided to become. You deserve someone who treats you like an empowered buyer, not just a commission check.

2. A Mortgage Lender Who Will Walk You Through Every Detail

You don't need someone who pushes you into the biggest loan possible. You need:

Clear breakdowns of costs and timelines

Guidance on loan options for your situation

Patience to help you build your understanding

3. People Who Encourage (Not Pressure) You

You may not have a big support system, and that's okay. But having at least one trusted voice-someone who reminds you that you're capable-can make a difference.

Even if you walk into every showing and closing alone, you don't have to carry the emotional weight alone. Your circle doesn't have to be big-it just has to be solid.

What I Wish Someone Had Told Me

Looking back, here are things I wish had been clearly explained:

The true costs of repairs and maintenance

How to evaluate a neighborhood beyond price

The importance of a detailed inspection

How to speak up if something didn't feel right

You don't know what you don't know-and that's why the people around you must be willing to tell you the truth.

If You're Going It Alone

You might be like me-strong, independent, used to figuring things out on your own. If so, here's my advice:

Educate yourself before you sign anything

Interview your agent and lender like you're hiring them (because you are)

Write down your goals and budget-and stick to them

Ask every question, even if you think it's silly

You deserve to feel informed, empowered, and confident every step of the way.

Why This Chapter Matters

Buying a home alone taught me more than I ever imagined. It led to regret, reflection, and ultimately reinvention. But it doesn't have to be that way for you.

This chapter isn't about telling you what to do-it's about making sure you know what to ask, who to trust, and how to protect yourself in a process that's full of emotion and financial weight.

You don't need a crowd-but you do need clarity.

And now, you've got someone in your corner.

Next up: In Chapter 7, we'll cover what happens after the closing-the real-life logistics of moving in, setting up your space, and claiming your new home with confidence.

Chapter 7: The Full Journey-From Pre-Approval to Keys

Everything That Happens-and When-During the Homebuying Process

Buying a home isn't just about making an offer and signing some papers. It's a process-a timeline with many steps that can feel overwhelming if you don't know what to expect. When I bought my home, I thought I had done everything right. But because I didn't understand the process fully, I made some decisions I later regretted.

That's why I'm giving you what I wish I had: a simple, honest roadmap of what happens from the very beginning-before you even see a house-all the way through to the moment you get the keys.

Step-by-Step Home Buying Timeline

✓Step 1: Get Pre-Qualified vs. Pre-Approved

Pre-Qualified: A quick estimate of what you might afford, often based on self-reported information. It's helpful for early planning but not as reliable when you're ready to shop.

Pre-Approved: A lender reviews your actual financial documents and gives you a letter stating how much you can borrow. This is what sellers and agents will expect when you make an offer.

Always get pre-approved-not just pre-qualified-before house hunting seriously.

Step 2: Gather Your Documents for Pre-Approval Be ready to provide:

Two most recent pay stubs

Two years of W-2s or tax returns (for self-employed)

Bank statements (last 2 months)

Photo ID

Social Security number for a credit check

Any documentation of assets or liabilities

Step 3: Understand What the Lender Looks For The underwriter evaluates your:

Credit score

Debt-to-income (DTI) ratio: This is the percentage of your monthly income that goes toward debt payments (including the new mortgage). A lower ratio (under 43%) is ideal.

Income and employment history

Assets/reserves (savings, 401k, etc.)

Once approved, you'll receive a pre-approval letter to include with offers.

Step 4: Start House Hunting and Make an Offer

With your pre-approval in hand:

Tour homes with your agent

Choose the one that fits your needs and budget

Make an offer with the agent's help Your offer may include:

Offer price

- Contingencies (financing, inspection, appraisal, etc.)
- Earnest money deposit (shows good faith, held in escrow)
- Timeline for inspections and closing

Step 5: Offer Is Accepted-Now What?

This triggers several things:

- Schedule a home inspection (usually within 7-10 days)
- Submit a formal mortgage application
- The lender orders an appraisal (to confirm the home's value)

Step 6: The Inspection and Appraisal

Home Inspection: Reveals potential issues. You can negotiate repairs, credits, or walk away (if your contract includes an inspection contingency).

Appraisal: If the home appraises for less than the offer, your options are:

- Renegotiating the price
- Pay the difference out-of-pocket
- Walk away if your contract allows

⚠ This is where a knowledgeable agent can truly protect you.

Step 7: Loan Goes to Underwriting

The underwriter re-checks your finances and home details. They may ask for:

Updated documents

Letters of explanation (for credit or income gaps)

Once they're satisfied, you get "clear to close."

Step 8: Receive Closing Disclosure (3 Days Before Closing) You'll receive a Closing Disclosure with all final numbers:

Loan amount

Interest rate

Monthly payment

Closing costs

Total funds needed to close

✨You must receive this at least 3 business days before closing.

Step 9: Closing Day Who's at the table:

You

Your agent (optional)

The title/escrow officer

Sometimes the seller or their rep You'll:

Show ID

Sign all loan and legal documents

Provide funds (cashier's check or wire transfer)

Step 10: When Do You Get the Keys?

If it's in your contract, you usually get them at closing or once the deed is recorded, often the same day.

Some contracts allow sellers to stay a few extra days (called a "rent-back"). Always clarify before closing.

⛉ What to Do Before Moving In

Change locks

Set up/transfer utilities

Update your address

Schedule movers

Notify banks, doctors, employers

Make a list of priority repairs

Now that you understand the full process from pre-approval to possession, the rest of Chapter 8 will help you settle in confidently

Chapter 8: After Closing - Settling In and Owning with Confidence

Now That You've Got the Keys, Here's What Comes Next

By now, you've walked through every step of the process-from pre-approval to appraisal, from contingencies to closing. And finally, you've made it: you have the keys in hand, and the home is yours.

But owning a home comes with a new chapter of responsibilities-and rewards. Whether you're moving immediately or taking a few days to prepare, this is your moment to breathe, reset, and make this space your own.

Your Move-In Checklist

Here's what to tackle right after closing:

Change the Locks

Even if the seller handed over all the keys they had, you don't know who else might have had access-contractors, former roommates, or neighbors. Schedule a locksmith or rekey the locks yourself.

Transfer Utilities Into Your Name Call or visit the websites for:

Gas

Electric

Water & Sewer

Trash collection

Internet & cable

Set your start date as the day of closing, so there's no interruption in service.

Change Your Address Update your address with:

The USPS (forwarding request)

Banks and credit cards

Voter registration

Social Security or Medicare

Insurance companies

Employer (payroll and W-2s)

Your doctor's office and pharmacy

✉Pro Tip: Create a list and check them off as you go. It's easy to miss something!

Clean and Prepare

Even if the house looks clean, doing your own "deep clean" before moving furniture helps you feel more settled and in control. Consider: Wiping cabinets and drawers

Shampooing carpets or mopping floors

Disinfecting bathrooms and kitchens

Replacing toilet seats and HVAC filters

What to Expect in the First 30 Days

Owning a home comes with maintenance and surprises. Keep a notebook or digital file to track:

Light repairs you want to make soon (sticky doors, loose tiles)

Big goals for the future (paint, landscaping, new appliances)

Your monthly utility bills and expenses

Start an emergency savings fund for unexpected repairs, even if you can only set aside $25-50/month. You're building long-term peace of mind.

œMake It Yours-One Corner at a Time

You don't have to decorate your entire house in one weekend. Focus on comfort first:

Set up your bedroom as a cozy retreat

Create a peaceful spot to unwind (a reading nook, a comfy chair, your favorite candle)

Hang one picture that makes you feel proud to be home

This isn't just a house-it's a reflection of your independence, your strength, and your future.

✦⁖Celebrate your journey. Take a photo on your front porch. Host a "soft" housewarming with one friend or your favorite dessert. You've earned it.

Give Yourself Grace

There will be moments of joy-and moments of doubt. You might feel overwhelmed, especially if you bought it alone. That's normal.

Remind yourself:

I don't have to do everything at once.

Every step I take is building my foundation.

This home is a reflection of how far I've come.

Final Thought for Chapter 7

You didn't just buy a house. You claimed a future. You made a decision that will ripple through your finances, your health, and your sense of peace.

You are a homeowner.

You are resilient.

You are ready.

Coming up in Chapter 8: How to get the most out of your home after you've bought it-practically and financially.

Chapter 9: Making the Most of Your Home

Turning Your House Into Opportunity, Comfort, and Cash Flow

Owning a home isn't just about having a roof over your head-it's about creating possibilities. Once you've settled in, your home becomes more than shelter. It can become a source of income, peace, pride, and even retirement planning.

I didn't know any of this when I first bought my house. But now I do-and I want to pass that knowledge on to you.

This chapter is all about how to get the most value, joy, and use out of your new home-whether that means growing your savings or growing your own tomatoes.

Build Equity and Use It Wisely

Equity is the difference between what your home is worth and what you still owe on your mortgage. As you pay down your loan-and as your home's value increases-you build equity.

Here's how to use it to your advantage:

Home Equity Loan or Line of Credit (HELOC): Borrow against your equity for large expenses like renovations or emergencies.

Refinancing: If rates drop or your credit improves, refinancing can lower your payments or loan terms.

Sell or downsize later: If your home's value rises, you may sell it years from now for a profit and move into something smaller or more affordable.

Equity builds wealth over time. Treat it with care-it's one of the biggest advantages of owning versus renting.

Rent Out a Room for Extra Income

You don't need a second property to generate rental income. If you have:

A spare bedroom

A finished basement

A separate entryway or bathroom

...you may be able to rent it out long-term or short-term (depending on your local laws and zoning).

Benefits:

Extra income can cover your mortgage, bills, or savings

You get to set the rules

It allows you to share space on your terms

Start with someone you trust or list through a verified platform.

Try Airbnb or Short-Term Rentals

Got a guest room or finished attic? You might be able to list it on platforms like Airbnb or Vrbo for occasional guests-especially if you live near a hospital, university, or event space.

⚠Check your city's regulations first. Some areas require permits or limit how many nights you can rent.

Tips to succeed:

Provide fresh linens and a clean, cozy space

Include basics like Wi-Fi, coffee, towels

Keep communication professional and prompt

You don't have to become a full-time host. Even one weekend a month could bring in a few hundred dollars.

Understand Reverse Mortgages (If You're 62+)

A reverse mortgage lets older homeowners convert part of their home's equity into cash-without selling or making monthly payments. It's not for everyone, but it can be useful if:

You have substantial equity

You need additional income in retirement

You plan to stay in your home long-term

Always speak with a certified housing counselor before considering a reverse mortgage.

There are pros, cons, and long-term implications.

Plant a Garden-Grow More Than Food

Even if you're not looking to make money from your home, you can make it a place of beauty and peace.

Benefits of gardening:

Reduces stress

Encourages healthy eating

Builds a sense of pride and purpose

Adds curb appeal and value to your property

You don't need a big yard. Start with:

Potted herbs on your porch

A raised bed for tomatoes or greens

A small flower garden to brighten your entryway

This isn't just about aesthetics-it's about claiming your space and making it reflect you.

Other Small but Powerful Ways to Enrich Your Home

Host workshops or gatherings: Turn your space into a place of connection

Set up a crafting or art corner: Fuel your creativity

Create a wellness space: A meditation area, home gym, or quiet nook

Start a home-based business: Whether it's jewelry, baking, or consulting

Final Thoughts

This is your home-but it's also your asset, your retreat, and your launchpad.

You've done the hard part. You made the leap into ownership. Now you get to enjoy it, build on it, and explore what's possible.

Use your home to:

Create peace

Build income

Express yourself and Empower your future

It's not just a house.

It's your investment.

It's your sanctuary.

It's yours.

Appendices

Appendix A: Homebuyer Glossary - Common Real Estate Terms

Appraisal

An independent assessment of a property's market value, usually done by a licensed appraiser, to ensure the home is worth the price being paid - especially for mortgage approval.

Buyer's Agent

A real estate agent who represents the buyer's interests in the transaction, helping with home searches, negotiations, and contract details.

Closing Costs

Fees paid at the end of a real estate transaction. They can include title insurance, appraisal fees, taxes, and lender charges. Typically range from 2% to 5% of the purchase price.

Contingency

A condition in the contract that must be met for the sale to proceed. Common examples include home inspection, financing, and appraisal contingencies.

Down Payment

The portion of the home's purchase price that the buyer pays upfront. This is separate from the loan. It can range from 3% to 20% or more, depending on the loan type.

Earnest Money

A deposit the buyer makes when submitting an offer to show they are serious. It's usually 1% to 3% of the purchase price and is applied to the buyer's closing costs if the deal goes through.

Escrow

A neutral third party that holds funds or documents until all parts of the real estate deal are completed.

Home Inspection

A professional examination of the home's condition - including roof, plumbing, electrical, HVAC, and structure - that helps the buyer understand potential issues before finalizing the sale.

Interest Rate

The cost of borrowing money, expressed as a percentage. The lower your rate, the less you'll pay over the life of your loan.

Loan-to-Value (LTV) Ratio

A percentage that compares your loan amount to the home's appraised value. A lower LTV typically means better loan terms and less risk for lenders.

Loan Estimate

A document from the lender that breaks down the loan terms, estimated payments, interest rate, and closing costs. It must be provided within 3 business days of applying for a loan.

Mortgage

A loan from a bank or lender used to buy a home. It includes the loan amount, interest, and term (usually

15-30 years).

Pre-Approval

A lender's written estimate of how much you can borrow, based on your financial info. It shows sellers you're a serious and qualified buyer.

Principal

The amount of money you borrow, not including interest. Each monthly mortgage payment includes a portion that goes toward reducing the principal.

Private Mortgage Insurance (PMI)

Insurance the lender may require if your down payment is less than 20%. It protects the lender in case you default on the loan.

Title

A legal document that proves who owns the property. A title search ensures there are no legal claims or liens on the home before closing.

Underwriting

The process where the lender reviews your financial information to decide whether to approve your loan.

Debt-to-Income (DTI) Ratio

A measure of how much of your monthly income goes toward debt. It helps lenders determine your ability to manage mortgage payments.

Walkthrough (Final Walkthrough)

A last visit to the home before closing to ensure it's in the agreed-upon condition and that repairs (if any) have been made.

Appendix B: Basic Homebuyer Budget Worksheet

Step 1: Monthly Income

Step 2: Monthly Expenses

Essential Expenses

Debt Payments

Step 3: Estimated Homeownership Costs

Step 4: Savings Snapshot

☑ Step 5: Can You Afford It?

Your Monthly Income: $_____

Minus Total Expenses & Debts: $_____

Estimated Monthly Home Costs: $_____

☐ I can comfortably afford the estimated monthly home costs.

☐ I may need to adjust my budget or save more before buying.

Appendix C: First-Time Homebuyer Checklist

Use this guide to track your progress from dreaming to moving in!

✓1. Prepare Your Finances

☐Check your credit report and score

☐Pay down debts and avoid new credit during the process

☐Start saving for down payment and closing costs

☐Create a monthly budget (see Budget Worksheet)

☐Get pre-approved by a mortgage lender

☐Understand your debt-to-income (DTI) ratio

✓2. Build Your Team

☐Choose a trusted real estate agent

☐Ask friends or family for referrals

☐Interview agents about experience, communication, and local knowledge

☐Start a folder for all documents and notes

✓3. Search for Your Home

☐Define your needs vs. wants (bedrooms, yard, location, etc.)

☐Research neighborhoods, school districts, taxes, and amenities

☐Attend showings and open houses

- ☐ Take notes and photos of each property you view

✓ **4. Make an Offer**

- ☐ Choose the right home and discuss offer terms with your agent
- ☐ Submit earnest money deposit
- ☐ Include contingencies (inspection, financing, appraisal)
- ☐ Negotiate if needed

✓ **5. Complete Inspections & Appraisal**

- ☐ Schedule a home inspection
- ☐ Review inspection report and request repairs (if needed)
- ☐ Home is appraised by lender to confirm market value
- ☐ Finalize terms with seller

✓ **6. Finalize Your Mortgage**

- ☐ Submit final documents to lender (taxes, pay stubs, bank statements)
- ☐ Go through underwriting (lender verifies your qualifications)
- ☐ Review and sign the Loan Estimate and closing disclosure
- ☐ Lock in your interest rate

✓ **7. Prepare for Closing Day**

- ☐ Complete a final walkthrough of the home

☐ Get a certified check or wire funds for closing

☐ Bring ID and all needed paperwork

☐ Sign all final documents at the closing table

✓ 8. After Closing

☐ Get keys and move in!

☐ Change address with USPS, bank, and important contacts

☐ Set up utilities in your name

☐ Test smoke detectors, change locks, and update security

☐ Register children in school (if applicable)

☐ Start your journey as a homeowner!

www.ingramcontent.com/pod-product-compliance
Lightning Source LLC
LaVergne TN
LVHW051925060526
838201LV00062B/4689